Buxton
Goyt Valley

Louise Maskill

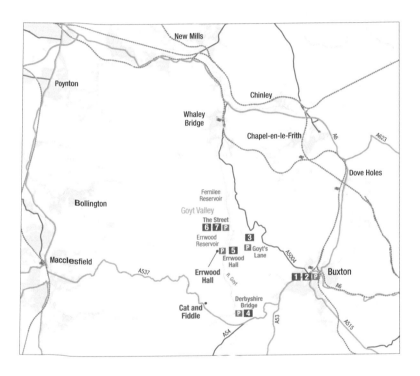

CURLEW
PRESS

Published by Curlew Press
Derbyshire

Email: mail@curlewpress.co.uk

British Library Cataloguing in Publication Data: a catalogue record for this book is available from the British Library.

1st Edition

ISBN: 978-1-9161044-5-7

Print – Short Run Press Ltd, Exeter, England

Text – Louise Maskill   **Walks** – Karl Barton

Design and layout – Mark Titterton

Photographs – Mark Titterton, except p.7 left, p.8 bottom left, p.41, p.47 top left (Karl Barton) and p.44 top (Sean O'Meara)

Archive Photographs – David Stirling (Gerald Hancock Collection) – p.33 bottom right, p.35 both, p.53 top. Curlew Press Collection – all others.

Maps – © OpenStreetMap Contributors (openstreetmap.org)
Contains OS data © Crown copyright and database right (2021)

Key to the maps in this book

······	Footpath	——	Track/former route or road	**i**	Visitor Information
•••••	Walking route		Route/road now below the reservoir	**P**	Parking
——	Trunk road	········	Railway	**WC**	Public toilets
——	A road		River		Grid: 1 mile square
——	B road		Demolished building		Contours: 10 metres
	Minor road		Extant building		Park/golf course
——	Service road	Stonway Quarry	Site of interest (demolished or extant)		Wood/plantation

About the Walks

The walks in this book are suitable for the reasonably fit, ranging in distance between 3½ and 7 miles. Some routes will take you over moorland footpaths, as well as across fields and through woodland; sturdy walking boots and appropriate clothing are essential. Weather conditions can be checked online at www.metoffice.gov.uk. While the maps in this guide are accurate, they are intended to be used in conjunction with a detailed Ordnance Survey map, such as the OS Explorer OL 24 (1:25 000 scale) covering the White Peak area.

Contents

The Peak District, Buxton and the Goyt Valley   4

Buxton   6

Location and geology   6
Ancient history   6
The Devonshires and spa tourism   7
The Pavilion Gardens and Serpentine Walks   10
Other notable buildings   12
Industrial history   12
Transport links   14
Notable visitors and residents   14
Buxton today   16

Walk 1: Buxton – Grinlow Woods and Solomon's Temple   18

Walk 2: Buxton – Corbar Cross   22

The Goyt Valley   28

Introduction   28
Location and geology   29
Ancient history   30
Industrial history   30
Transport links   33
The Grimshawes and Errwood Hall   35
The Errwood and Fernilee Reservoirs   37
The Goyt Valley today   38

Walk 3: Goyt's Lane - Burbage   40

Walk 4: Derbyshire Bridge, Cat and Fiddle and Goytsclough   45

Walk 5: Errwood Hall   50

Walk 6: The Street – The Tors   54

Walk 7: The Street – Taxal   59

Bibliography   64

The Peak District, Buxton and the Goyt Valley

The Peak District forms the southern extremity of the Pennine Hills, the backbone of England that stretches northwards through Yorkshire and Cumbria as far as the Tyne Gap. The Peak District National Park was the first in England and Wales, created in 1951 and including parts of Derbyshire, Cheshire, Greater Manchester, Staffordshire, and West and South Yorkshire.

The Peaks have a fascinating history of settlement, industry, agriculture and tradition, and the area has welcomed visitors for centuries. Its name stems not from the hilly landscape – in fact there are few true peaks in the Peak District, with most of the hills having flat or rounded summits – but rather from the Pecsaetan (Old English: 'peak-dwellers'), probably a tribe of Anglo-Saxon invaders who displaced the native Brigantes during the 6th century AD.

The geology of the area is divided into two distinct sections; the gritstone and shale Dark Peak (or High Peak) forms an inverted horseshoe to the west, north and east, while the limestone White Peak constitutes the central and

southern areas. The Dark Peak is higher, wilder and more sparsely populated and includes the rugged heights of Kinder Scout and Mam Tor, while the White Peak is known for its steep-sided dales and limestone edges, but both areas contains gentler pockets of habitation and agricultural land. One such is the Goyt Valley, five miles to the west of the spa town of Buxton.

Buxton stands at the boundary between the Dark and White Peak geological areas, a fact that accounts for the warm springs that made the town famous. Their thermal properties were exploited as far back as the Romans, bringing periods of fame and prosperity to the town. Meanwhile, the Goyt Valley has a centuries-long history of agriculture and small industry, but the biggest change in its character came in the 20th century with the damming of the River Goyt to form the Errwood and Fernilee Reservoirs.

This book will introduce you to the history, people and stories of Buxton and the Goyt Valley, and offers a selection of carefully curated circular walks so you can discover the area for yourself. You'll meet Georgian aristocrats and Victorian industrialists, highwaymen and monarchs as you explore these fascinating corners of Derbyshire.

The Goyt Valley

5

Buxton

Location and geology

High on the Derbyshire moors at just over 1,000 feet above sea level, the market town of Buxton has attracted visitors for centuries. The local climate is famously rainy and bracing, but it has always been an important regional centre for trade and tourism, and was favoured by the Romans, the Georgians and the Victorians for its health-giving thermal waters.

The warm springs rise at a constant temperature of 27.7°C (82°F), emerging at the boundary between deposits of limestone and gritstone upon which the town sits. There are nine warm springs and one chalybeate (iron-bearing) spring, all of which were used for therapeutic purposes at various times, although most are now capped and diverted into the River Wye.

Ancient history

The earliest evidence of habitation in the Buxton area dates from the Stone Age; traces of Mesolithic and Neolithic settlements were found in Lismore Fields, with 6,000-year-old cereal stores suggesting the earliest stages of the transition from hunter-gatherers to settled farming. The fragmented 'Lismore Pot', on display in Buxton Museum, is thought to be 5,500 years old, one of the oldest ever found in Britain.

The Romans knew Buxton well; they called it *Aquae Arnemetiae*, the Waters of the Goddess of the Grove, and continued the local Celtic tradition of honouring the deity of the springs. They built roads, a temple, a forum and a market place, and a large bathing complex so that visitors could take advantage of the thermal waters.

The Roman settlement was abandoned in the 5th century AD when the legions withdrew from Britain, but the reputation of the springs endured and they became a local pilgrimage site. The medieval St Anne's Well was attracting pilgrims seeking healing during the dissolution of the monasteries in the 1530s, and the first medical treatise on the health-giving waters was written around 1572 by Dr John Jones. Buxton's health tourism business was beginning to grow, with the waters reputed to ease stiffened and inflamed joints, as well as being effective for uterine, kidney and digestive afflictions.

Opposite left: Stained glass window inside the Pump Room depicting St Anne
Opposite right: St Anne's drinking well during the 1920s

The Devonshires and spa tourism

Buxton's main business of attracting invalids to take the waters was largely driven by the Cavendish family, later the Dukes of Devonshire, who began to acquire property in the town during the 16th century. At that time Buxton was remote, difficult to get to and uncomfortable once one arrived, but the waters were thought to be so efficacious that many endured these hardships for the sake of a cure.

The initially primitive bathing facilities were modernised during the 17th and 18th centuries, and by the time the Georgian Crescent and Great Stables were built by the 5th Duke of Devonshire in the 1780s Buxton had become a fashionable spa resort rivalling Bath in popularity. As well as therapeutic treatments the town boasted hotels, boarding houses, shopping arcades, a racecourse and other entertainments – it was a place for the aristocracy to see and be seen.

By the middle of the 19th century it was estimated that the Devonshire estate owned 80% of the township, with facilities to entertain around 13,000 guests annually. By this time, however, the focus had shifted from fashionable spa tourism to the medical mainstream; the Victorians were notoriously health-conscious, and the hydropathic water treatments in Buxton were backed by eminent medical professionals. Middle-class Victorians flocked to Buxton to take cold and warm baths, be massaged and douched, and drink the slightly sulphurous or metallic-tasting waters.

Growth continued with the arrival of the railways in 1863, with lines north to Manchester and south to Derby offering much easier access for visitors. By the start of the 20th century Buxton was at its apogee, with 27 hotels and 300 lodging houses catering for 4,000 visitors weekly at the height of the season. Hydro hotels opened year-round to offer winter sports, and the Devonshire Hospital (converted from the Great Stables in 1859 by the addition of the magnificent Devonshire Dome) was a national centre for hydrotherapy, rheumatology and orthopædics.

Top: The exterior of the iconic Crescent **Left:** The Georgian splendour of the grand Assembly Room inside the Crescent Hotel **Middle:** The Crescent in the early 1900s **Right:** The Devonshire Dome

However, many hydros were converted into hospitals or billets during World War I, and hydrotherapy declined in popularity during the inter-war years. During the second half of the 20th century most of the hydros were demolished or converted to other uses, although the Devonshire Hospital (from 1935 the Devonshire Royal Hospital) stayed open until 2000, with its hydrotherapy pools in use right to the end.

Part of the Crescent remained a hotel, with other sections of the building used as a hospital, council offices and the town's library. It closed in 1992 because of structural problems, but along with the Baths it has recently undergone a major renovation into a luxury spa hotel.

The Pavilion Gardens

The Octagon

The Pavilion Gardens and Serpentine Walks

The construction of the Crescent in the 1780s and the proliferation of other spa hotels created a need for outdoor exercise areas for the recovering guests. The riverside Serpentine Walks were created at this time, and other amenities were provided on an area of land once belonging to the Old Hall. The public area that would become the Pavilion Gardens had been born.

In 1857 J.C. Bates, proprietor and editor of the Buxton Advertiser, noted the need for '*a large building, where music, exercise and social converse can easily be enjoyed*'. This became more pressing as Buxton's expansion continued, and in 1870 the 7th Duke of Devonshire donated a further 9 acres of land. By 1871 the first Pavilion building had been erected, designed by Edward Milner who had assisted Joseph Paxton with London's Crystal Palace. The original Pavilion was a central hall with two Conservatories heated by hot water pipes, offering a sheltered place to listen to bands and walk in inclement weather. However, high admission charges excluded local residents, who were incensed about the '*shutting-up of the Pleasure-Grounds which have been free from time immemorial*'.

The octagonal Concert Hall was added in 1876, designed by the local architect Robert Rippon Duke. Another 11 acres of land were added in 1880, and by 1883 the gardens boasted a reading room, a smoking room, a roller-skating rink, and a boating lake offering ice-skating in winter.

The Entertainment Stage (later the Playhouse) opened in the 1880s, and an ornate Oriental Tea Kiosk in 1899. A grand entrance to the gardens was erected in 1903 to coincide with the opening of Frank Matcham's magnificent Opera House, with the first silent film shown there in 1921.

The Oriental Tea Kiosk, c.1940s

During the mid-20th century the town rebranded as a conference centre, the Opera House began to host drama festivals, and the Concert Hall continued in regular use as a ballroom and dance hall (hosting the Beatles in 1962 and 1963). However, spa tourism had all but died, and the relatively small venues in the town began to lose out to larger concert halls elsewhere. The entrance fee to the Gardens was abolished in the early 1970s, the Concert Hall was threatened with demolition, and the Oriental Tea Kiosk was lost.

The birth of Buxton Opera Festival in 1979 heralded a resurgence in the town's fortunes. The Playhouse was remodelled into the Paxton Suite in 1980, and the Conservatory was restored in 1982. A serious fire damaged the Concert Hall and Pavilion in 1983, but the resulting restoration is generally agreed to be an improvement on the previous arrangements. The Pavilion Arts Centre was created in 2010.

Today the Pavilion Gardens offers shopping, an art gallery, an ice cream parlour, the Octagon concert hall, the Arts Centre (including a cinema run by Buxton Film) and a restaurant and tea rooms, along with the Serpentine Walks, lakes, bandstand, playgrounds, and even an outdoor gym. Among other things it hosts dramatic and musical performances, antique and collectors' fairs and classic car auctions; its survival is testament to investment by the town over many years, and support and use by generations of local residents and visitors.

Other notable buildings

The terraced gardens on St Ann's Cliff, known as the Slopes, were laid out in 1818 by Jeffry Wyatville and later modified by Joseph Paxton. Along with the Serpentine Walks and the Pavilion Gardens, they provided outdoor exercise grounds for invalids staying in the town's therapeutic establishments, with patients attempting longer and steeper walks as their health improved; this was known as the 'Terrain Cure', and was one of Buxton's unique offerings.

The Pump Room, facing the Crescent, was designed by Henry Currey and opened in 1894 to provide an elegant social space where visitors could take the waters. It was last used for this purpose in the 1970s, later housing a Micrarium and then standing empty for a number of years. It has recently been refurbished as part of the Crescent renovation, and now houses Buxton's Tourist Information Centre in grand style.

The healing reputation of St Anne's Well has attracted visitors to Buxton since medieval times, but an Enclosure Act of 1772 also stipulates that there must always be a source of the town's spring water available free to local residents, kept clean and in good repair. The current St Anne's Well, near the Pump Room at the foot of the Slopes, continues to serve this function, dating from 1940 and known locally as the Lion's Head. The well was originally housed in a much earlier structure nearer the Baths, being moved to its present site during the construction of the Crescent in the 1780s.

St Anne's Church in Higher Buxton dates from the 17th century, but it is thought to incorporate fabric from a much older building and therefore to be the oldest building in Buxton. The Church of St John the Baptist, over the road from the Pavilion Gardens, was designed by Wyatville and built in 1811 by the 6th Duke of Devonshire; Anne Lister described it in 1816 as '*one of the neatest and most beautiful little buildings of the kind I ever saw*'.

Industrial history

Buxton's spas played a significant role in the town's development, but they were by no means the only source of revenue. The town is at the western edge of the Peak District's limestone plateau, and limestone has been quarried in the area for centuries. Lime is produced by the heating and slaking (rapid cooling with water) of limestone, and was used in the manufacture of mortar and as a soil improver.

Grin Low was the earliest centre of limeworking in the Buxton area, owned by the Devonshire estate and licensed for lime burning from the 17th century. The remains of over 100 lime kilns dot the landscape along with the remains of the lime-burners' troglodytic dwellings, hollowed out from hardened and compacted spoil heaps. The hill overlooks the town and must have been something of an

Left: Colonnade around The Square in the town's conservation area **Right:** St Anne's Well or the Lion's Head

eyesore; in the 1820s the 6th Duke of Devonshire commissioned the planting of the Grin Low Plantation (now the Buxton Country Park) to provide tree cover and hide the scarred landscape from visitors to the fashionable spa resort.

Many more quarries opened in the late 19th and early 20th centuries, prompted by the arrival of the railway and increased demand from industry. Buxton Lime Firms was formed by a number of competing quarry owners in 1891, and in 1926 Buxton became the headquarters of the Lime Division of the newly-formed ICI. Although the last quarry on Grin Hill closed in 1952, limestone extraction in the Buxton area continues today, with active quarries in Sterndale Moor and Topley Pike and the enormous 'Tunstead Superquarry' in Great Rocks Dale. A Hoffman Kiln, a new type of kiln patented by the German inventor Friedrich Hoffman in 1858, was built by the Buxton Lime Company adjacent to the quarry at Harpur Hill in 1872, and continued to produce lime there until it was decommissioned in 1944.

The town was also a centre for working and retailing Ashford Black Marble, a dark limestone found near Ashford-in-the-Water. This was driven by the Victorian passion for souvenirs; the black stone can be cut, turned and polished to a high shine, and in Buxton it was used to make urns, obelisks, paperweights, jewellery and other decorative objects for visitors to purchase. It was also used in architectural and structural objects such as fireplaces and tables, often inlaid with coloured stones such as Blue John and yellow fluorspar. Buxton Museum houses a fine collection acquired from the Tomlinson family, who once owned an inlaying workshop in the town.

Transport links

The roads around Buxton have been famously difficult through much of its history. The Romans were the first to tackle the problem of building roads over the challenging moorland; the best preserved of these are Batham Gate, between Buxton and the fort of Navio to the northeast, and The Street that connected Buxton with a possible fort at Carsington and the settlement of Derventio, in Derby.

After the legions departed their roads fell into disrepair and travel became increasingly difficult, particularly for wheeled vehicles, but the Turnpike Acts of the 18th and 19th centuries allowed private investors to build toll roads in an effort to boost industry and trade. Derbyshire benefited significantly from this initiative, and the Buxton to Manchester turnpike was the earliest in the county, opening in 1725.

More turnpikes followed, with routes from Buxton to Sheffield and Buxton to Macclesfield in 1759. Even after better roads were constructed, however, travel around Buxton was still notoriously challenging; the diarist Anne Lister travelled from Macclesfield to Buxton in 1816 and described the road as '*a series of tremendously ups and downs through the wildest moor country imaginable*'.

The railway arrived in Buxton in June 1863 with two adjacent stations, both designed by Sir Joseph Paxton with matching rose window façades. They were operated by the London and North Western Railway (providing a direct line to Manchester via Whaley Bridge) and the Midland Railway (giving access to the London main line via Rowsley and a branch line at Millers Dale). This provided much easier access for paying guests and day trippers from all directions, who were possibly the most significant factor in the town's rapid growth.

The Midland station closed in 1967 and much of the building was removed, although parts of the line remain as freight routes. Paxton's original rose window in the façade of the LNWR station was restored in 2009.

Notable visitors and residents

George Talbot, 6th Earl of Shrewsbury, developed the New Hall (now the Old Hall Hotel) in 1572/3 as a lodge for himself and his guests when they visited Buxton, and also as a secure house for Mary Queen of Scots, then a prisoner of the Crown. Mary visited Buxton a number of times between 1573 and 1584 to take the waters to ease the pain of rheumatism or arthritis; she was Shrewsbury's captive on the orders of her cousin Queen Elizabeth I, who was convinced (perhaps not without foundation) that the Scottish Queen was a threat to her throne.

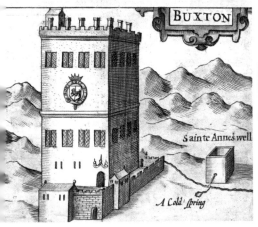 

Left: The New Hall, depicted on John Speed's (1610) map of Derbyshire **Right:** The Old Hall Hotel

Mary's tragic fate is well known; she was executed at Fotheringhay in 1587. On one of her final visits to Buxton she is said to have left a prophetic inscription on a window pane in the Old Hall:

> *Buxtona, quae calidae celebraris nomine Lymphae,*
> *Forte mihi post hoc non adeunda, Vale!*
>
> *Buxton, whose fame thy milk-warm waters tell,*
> *Whom I, perhaps, no more shall see, Farewell!*

The 19th century Yorkshire diarist Anne Lister visited Buxton in 1816 on a journey to Cheshire, and then again in 1824, this time for seven weeks with her aunt who was taking the waters. Anne's diaries give a vivid picture of the town at that time; she reports that the baths were rather disappointing – '*dark low places, the dressing rooms … very small, and seemingly uncomfortable. There is only one public bath for the ladies and one for the gents – one private bath for the ladies and one for the gents*'.

Buxton has produced a number of famous residents. Vera Brittain lived in Buxton Park between 1904 and 1950; she was a pacifist and feminist, working in the Devonshire Hospital as a VAD (Voluntary Aid Detachment) nurse during World War I. She was later famous for her autobiographical book *Testament of Youth*, a feminist account of World War I and its devastating impact on her loved ones and society.

Robert Stevenson, the director of classic Disney films such as *Mary Poppins* and *Bedknobs and Broomsticks*, was born in Buxton in 1905. The influential singer/songwriter Lloyd Cole was born here in 1961, and Tim Brooke-Taylor, one third of the Goodies and a much loved (and much missed) comedian, was born in the town in 1940.

Left: The Opera House

Opposite left: Well dressing, 2021

Opposite right: The Cavendish Shopping Arcade, formerly the Thermal Baths

Buxton today

The fashion for health tourism faded in the early 20th century and Buxton's fortunes suffered a dip, but the town is currently undergoing a revival with the multi-million-pound development of a luxury spa complex in the Crescent. Although it is no longer part of the medical establishment, Buxton's mineral water also maintains its reputation as a healthy and natural drink, available free from St Anne's Well but also bottled locally and sold worldwide by Nestlé.

The town has always been a popular centre for walking and outdoor pursuits, ideally placed for exploring the surrounding Peak District National Park. For over 40 years Buxton has also attracted music and literature lovers to the Buxton International Festival. Centred on the Opera House, the festival has a reputation for staging rarely performed operatic works, and offers a year-round programme of literary, musical and dramatic entertainments including the Buxton Fringe open arts festival.

The fine natural limestone cave of Poole's Cavern, under Grin Low, has attracted visitors for centuries. Indeed, unlike some of rather more rugged show caves elsewhere, in the 19th century Poole's Cavern was lit and made accessible for invalid visitors, who could make the excursion in their bath chairs. The cave's name is said to derive from a medieval outlaw who made his hideout there, and there is evidence of habitation as far back as the Bronze Age.

Poole's Cavern is next to Buxton Country Park, including the 100-acre Grin Low Plantation created by the 6th Duke of Devonshire in the 1820s to mask the scars of limeworking. The park is an SSSI because of the birds and plants that thrive here, offering walking routes, a sculpture trail and the Victorian folly of Solomon's Temple on the summit of Grin Low. This distinctive tower dominates the skyline to the south of the town, commanding splendid views across the town and the surrounding countryside including Mam Tor and Kinder.

On the other side of the town are Corbar Woods, a surviving 54-acre patch of ancient woodland that puts on a spectacular display of bluebells in the spring. There are various routes through the woods to Corbar Cross, given to the town's Catholic congregation by the 10th Duke of Devonshire in 1950.

Well dressing is an ancient Peak District tradition perhaps dating back to pre-Christian times, celebrated by towns, villages and hamlets across the region. Communities come together to design and construct elaborate pictures from natural objects such as flower petals and seeds, which are then used to decorate local water sources. In Buxton the modern revival of this ancient tradition dates back to 1840, when the Devonshire estate installed piped fresh water to a public well in the town centre. Since then well dressing has been an annual event, now coinciding with the town's carnival in July.

Higher Buxton hosts a twice-weekly market in the Market Place on Tuesdays and Saturdays, with a variety of stalls and takeaway food vendors, and there are farmers' markets on the first Thursday of each month held in the Pavilion Gardens. Buxton Museum and Art Gallery are in the former Peak Hydropathic Hotel on Terrace Road. Recently refurbished, the museum houses geological, palæolontological, artistic and sociological collections related to Buxton and the surrounding area, and is well worth a visit.

Walk 1: Buxton – Grinlow Woods and Solomon's Temple

Essential Information

Start: The Market Place, Higher Buxton

Public Transport: Buses from Derby, Stockport, Glossop, Sheffield, Macclesfield, local towns and villages converge at Buxton Market Place. The railway station maintains a regular service, calling at stations to Manchester with onward connections nationwide.

Facilities: Toilets: Sylvan car and coach park, Market Place, Pavilion Gardens. Shops, pubs, cafés and restaurants throughout the town.

Car Park: Market Place, Market Street, Pavilion Gardens, Sylvan car and coach park.

Distance: 3 ½ miles

Path Description: Mostly urban roadside pavement; hard paths through woodland and footpaths over pasture and fields. Steady gradient to Solomon's Temple.

About the Walk

Buxton received its market charter in 1813, and we start this walk from the Market Place, the focal point of Higher Buxton. Following the A515 High Street we descend to the former Macclesfield turnpike via the narrow Church Street.

Taking to the residential streets, we thread our way towards Poole's Cavern, and then ascend through Buxton Country Park (formerly known as Grin Low Woods), which disguises the former industrial landscape created by lime quarrying and burning, to reach

Scrivener's Books, High Street

the pockmarked grassland that surrounds Solomon's Temple. Climb the tower for a fabulous panoramic view of the town and landscape beyond.

Descending the hillside, we pass the sites of long-demolished farms and cross the probable routes of two Roman roads before returning to the Market Place via the former cattle market. Though much of the walk is urban, stout footwear is recommended in order to negotiate the off-road terrain.

Directions

1. From the Market Place, head south to the western pavement of High Street, crossing Fountain Street and Chapel Street before the Market Place narrows to a parade of shops. Continue along High Street to Bath Road. In front of the Town Hall is the shaft of a cross, which has moved around the Market Place but was originally sited around St Anne's Stables several hundred yards away.

2. Cross Bath Road to take Church Street, between the Swan and Scrivener's Books and Bookbinding. Follow Church Street as it descends to West Road. The Swan, formerly the Shoulder of Mutton, is a listed late 18th century building. On the opposite side of High Street are the slightly older listed coaching inns, the Sun and the Cheshire Cheese. The church of St Anne, which lies alongside Church Street, has a stone engraved with the date 1625, making it the oldest church standing in the town; parts of the building are said to be even older.

3. At West Road, turn right for 60 yards. West Road formed part of the 1759 Buxton to Macclesfield turnpike; a few yards to your left, at Five Ways, there was once a toll house.

4. Take the first turn on your left signed "Leading to Trinity Stables", with Ashford House the first building on the right. Head up the short road and continue along the gennel (the narrow passage) at its head.

5. Turn right into Spencer Road, following it for less than 200 yards to its junction with College Road.

6. Turn right into College Road, gently descending the short distance to Temple Road on your left.

7. Turn left into Temple Road and follow it for a quarter of a mile to where it becomes Milldale Avenue.

8. Turn left to follow Temple Road a short distance to its junction with Green Lane.

9. Turn right, passing the entrance to Poole's Cavern on your left. Climb fairly steeply for 100 yards up Green Lane and then locate the footpath fingerpost on your left.

10. Turning back on yourself, take the footpath up the driveway, which soon becomes a wide and well-trodden earthen path. Continue through the woods without deviation for just shy of half a mile.

11. Emerging from the woods onto the scarred landscape of Grin Low, follow the path to Solomon's Temple (Grin Low Tower). The viewing platform of the tower is accessible and worth the short climb on a clear day.

Grin Low and Solomon's Temple

12. Take the path which descends a few yards directly from the doorway of the tower to a stile in the stone wall opposite.

13. Descend the pockmarked terrain to the boundary wall of High Plantation, passing the location of the former Temple Farm on your way. The farm was home to the Turner family, noted in the census returns between 1881 and 1911. Mary Hannah Turner was the head of household after the death of her husband Thomas in 1889.

14. In the wood the path descends to your right and continues within the tree line for around 220 yards.

15. Once over the dilapidated stile with the wood behind you, take the path at two o'clock, **not** the most well-trodden path that follows the wall on your left.

16. On the relatively flat surface of the playing fields, cross to the tree-lined track opposite.

17. Turn right along the track, which divides beyond the tree cover.

18. Keep left, crossing the meadow to Fern Road less than 300 yards away.

19. Turn left at Fern Road, following it the short distance to London Road.

20. Turn left into London Road, the busy A515, crossing at some point on the 170-yard stretch to Heath Grove.

21. Turn right into Heath Grove, formerly Recreation Road, for a few yards and cross to enter the recreation ground.

22. Cross the rec to Byron Street. Between numbers 20 and 21, which sports a plaque commemorating the "Best kept street winner 1996" and "A brighter Buxton initiative", is a gennel to New Market Street.

23. Pass along the gennel and New Market Street beyond down to the busy Dale Road (the B5059).

24. Cross Dale Road and follow Market Street some 270 yards back to the Market Place.

Walk 2: Buxton – Corbar Cross

Essential Information

Start: The Market Place, Higher Buxton

Public Transport: Buses from Derby, Stockport, Glossop, Sheffield, Macclesfield, local towns and villages converge at Buxton Market Place. The railway station maintains a regular service, calling at stations to Manchester with onward connections nationwide.

Facilities: Toilets: Sylvan car and coach park, Market Place, Pavilion Gardens. Shops, pubs, cafés and restaurants throughout the town.

Car Park: Market Place, Market Street, Pavilion Gardens, Sylvan car and coach park.

Distance: 4 miles

Path Description: Mostly urban roadside pavement; hard paths through woodland and footpaths over pasture and fields. Steady gradient to Corbar Cross.

Broad Walk

Bluebells in Corbar Woods

About the Walk

Starting from Buxton Market Place, we pass behind the Town Hall and descend The Slopes to the open space adjacent to the former Hot Baths. Enjoy the splendour of Buxton Crescent Hotel and the Pump Room opposite, which now houses the Buxton Visitor Centre, before passing St Anne's Well (the Lion's Head) and the Old Hall Hotel on your way to Broad Walk, which runs the length of the Pavilion Gardens. Cutting across the gardens, our route takes us through the Serpentine Walks, a similarly manicured area of urban parkland.

Crossing St John's Road we pass through Gadley Woods and beside Cavendish Golf Club. After a short stretch along Manchester Road we ascend to Corbar Cross, making our way around the boundary within the confines of Corbar Woods. Corbar Cross offers fine views across the town of Buxton, the Wye Valley and the moors towards Whaley Bridge, Dove Holes and Peak Forest.

Descending back to the urban environment, we make our way past the well-appointed dwellings lining Marlborough and Devonshire Roads to pass between the impressive Devonshire Dome and Palace Hotel.

Passing the remaining wall and fan window of the twin railway stations, the path takes us alongside the once-roofed platforms of the London and North Western Railway station and the former site of the depot that serviced the commuter trains and locomotives of the heavy limestone traffic originating in the area.

Lightwood Road and Charles Street take us through the previously industrial area of Hogshaw to walk close to the viaduct that dominates this part of town. This area once boasted Sylvan Park, which was intersected by the viaduct and included a bandstand within the area closest to town. We return to the Market Place via the precipitous Holker Road.

Directions

1. From the Market Place, take the narrow road to the immediate right of the Town Hall. Follow the road around the back of the Town Hall and into the car park.

2. Locate the multi-fingered sign post where the car park turns to the right. Follow the broad tree-lined avenue that descends to the Crescent opposite the Grove Hotel.

3. Turn left into the Crescent with Cavendish Arcade, Buxton Crescent (St Anne's) Hotel and the Old Hall Hotel on your right, and the Pump Room and St Anne's Well on your left.

4. At the junction with the Crescent, Hall Bank, Hartington Road, Broad Walk and the Square, follow Broad Walk 240 yards to where Fountain Street enters from the left.

5. Locate the multi-fingered sign post and follow the main path on your right to cross the Pavilion Gardens towards the Serpentine, crossing over and under a number of bridges.

6. Cross Burlington Road to enter the Serpentine, which is almost opposite the path you have just left. Follow the path through the park, exiting beside a road bridge on St John's Road, the A53.

7. Cross St John's Road with care, taking the path opposite that continues to follow the River Wye towards Gadley Lane.

8. Turn right into Gadley Lane, which is initially a metalled road.

9. As the road bears left, continue along the path ahead, which leads to a footbridge over the Wye. Cross the footbridge and follow the broad track up through Gadley Woods (formerly Brickyard Plantation) towards Cavendish Golf Club.

10. As the track becomes a metalled road once more, continue uphill with the clubhouse on your left and car park on the right.

11. Follow the path ahead for a little over 200 yards to Manchester Road, the A5004.

12. Turn right into Manchester Road and cross where possible, following the road downhill for 250 yards to the bus stop opposite The Gables.

13. Take the footpath on your left immediately after the bus stop, which rises to a gate some 150 yards away.

14. Beyond the gate, keep to the left-hand fork in the path which continues to rise, then follow the main path as it meanders around old quarry workings while rising steeply to a confluence of paths.

15. Keep left to follow the path heading for the westerly boundary of Corbar Woods around 200 yards away. The path curves around close to the western boundary wall while climbing steeply for approximately 100 yards, then follows the northern wall for 200 yards in an easterly direction towards a stile, permitting access to the field beyond.

16. Cross the field to a stile in the wall ahead.

17. Straight ahead the path climbs the rock outcrop, where you should turn left into the fenced enclosure surrounding Corbar Cross. If you are unsure about climbing the outcrop, take the path to your right which offers a more gentle approach to the cross.

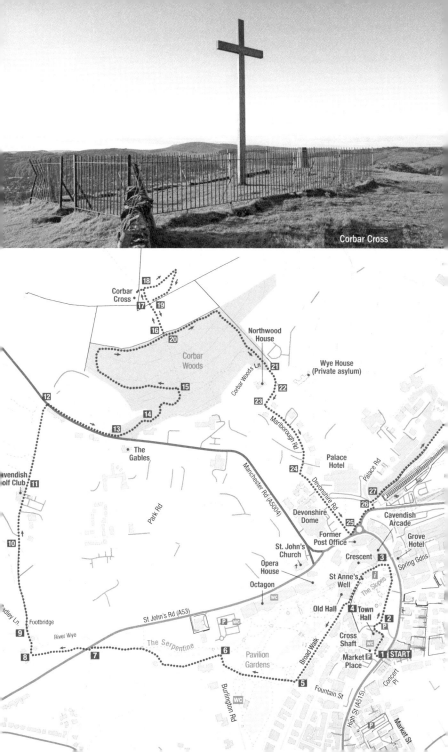

Corbar Cross

18. Exiting Corbar Cross enclosure, continue ahead with the cliff edge on your right, following the path as it winds around the outcrop back to the stile below.

19. Cross the field back to the stile into Corbar Woods.

20. Turn left and follow the path along the northern boundary wall of Corbar Woods. The path turns to the south-east as it approaches the boundary that steeply descends the hill. If you are unsure about negotiating this steep path, take the alternative route from the stile, which descends the hillside via steps. At the foot of these you should follow the path to your left.

21. Take the path ahead, descending via Corbar Woods Lane with Northwood House on your right to Corbar Road. To your left, opposite the end of Corbar Woods Lane, once stood Wye House Asylum, later Cavendish School; this was designed by Henry Currey, built in 1861 and demolished in 1990. The establishment catered for "the care and treatment of the insane of the higher and middle classes". Francis Kennedy Dickson, born in 1843 in Scotland, was the live-in proprietor and physician noted in the census returns of 1871 to 1901. Dr Dickson not only ran the asylum but was also a Senior Consulting Physician at the Devonshire Hospital and JP for the county of Derbyshire. He died in 1907.

22. Turn right into Corbar Road for 70 yards.

23. Turn left into Marlborough Road, following it down to the crossroads with Devonshire Road.

24. Turn left into Devonshire Road, which descends between the Palace Hotel on your left and the Devonshire Dome on your right. As you near the bottom of the road, notice the curved building ahead; this was once the Post Office, with carved stonework at roof height bearing testament to its former function.

25. Turn left opposite the old Post Office into Station Road, with views down the Quadrant on your right. Rising up Station Road, the fan window of the L&NW railway station is ahead of you, while the remains of the Midland station are visible on the opposite side of the road; a substantial stone wall of one corner of the former train shed survives.

26. Cross Palace Road to the left-most corner of the stone station wall.

27. Follow the footpath alongside Buxton station and the remains of the former maintenance depot. The path continues around the boundary of a row of cottages and descends beside the remains of a bridge abutment that once crossed Lightwood Road, formerly Hogshaw Lane.

28. Turn right, passing beneath the three surviving and well-used bridges, to reach the crossroads with Brooklands, Nunsfield Road and Charles Street, 200 yards ahead. On your left shortly beyond the bridges is Hogshaw Villas Road, which is lined by several railway cottages first noted in the 1881 census.

29. Turn right into Charles Street and pass beneath a further three railway bridges, the last of which was replaced by Peak Rail in the early 1990s but remains unused.

30. Keep left on Bridge Street, with the viaduct rising on your left.

31. Beneath the viaduct, cross the A53 to Sylvan car park, formerly Sylvan Park, and turn right, entering Spring Gardens for only a few yards.

Above: Joseph Paxton's fan window at the railway station

32. Turn left into Holker Road, passing the former White Lion on your right at the bottom of the hill. Holker Road rises steeply towards Higher Buxton; after less than 300 yards you reach the T junction with Silverlands. Beyond the junction with Clifton Road was the site of Higher Buxton goods yard (LNWR).

33. Turn right into Silverlands, which shortly becomes Hardwick Square South; here a plaque on the wall at The Mountlands records the location where a Roman milestone was found. Beyond is Concert Place.

34. Turn right into Market Street, which immediately returns you to the Market Place.

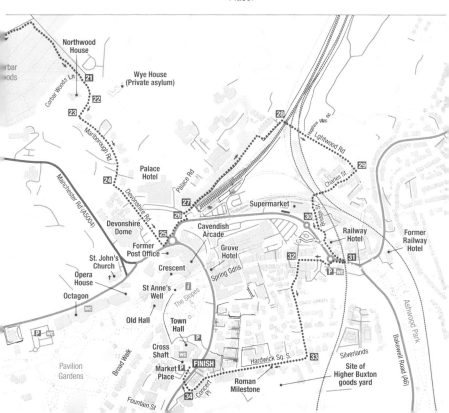

The Goyt Valley

Introduction

Although its immediate surroundings are rugged and remote, the gritstone Goyt Valley on the western edge of the Peak District National Park has always had a reputation as a beauty spot, although its aspect is much changed today compared with previous centuries. Tranquil, romantic and only six miles from the popular town of Buxton, the valley was popular among Victorian day-trippers, who visited the hamlet of Goyt's Bridge and walked by the river and over the stepping stones to visit tea rooms and farms.

The four-mile upper stretch of the valley contains a surprising range of terrains from high moorland to woodland and valleys, with the manmade additions of the Errwood and Fernilee Reservoirs alongside the evocative ruins of Errwood Hall. These days there is almost no permanent habitation, but the valley was once home to a thriving community, with a gunpowder factory, a railway, a paint mill and a Victorian mansion as well as scattered farms and homesteads. It remains popular with visitors today for its natural beauty as well as its amenities and history.

Location and geology

The River Goyt rises on Axe Edge Moor at the southern end of the valley between Whetstone Ridge and the Cat and Fiddle Inn, flowing initially eastward under the busy A537 between Buxton and Macclesfield and then turning northwards to follow the Upper Goyt Valley, being joined by tributaries channelled through deep rocky clefts such as Berry Clough and Shooters Clough. The valley is a syncline – a downward fold in the layers of limestone, shale and gritstone bedrock, laid down when the area was covered by a great river some 300 million years ago. The compressed layers were tilted and folded by earth movements, the exposed shales and grits were sculpted by successive Ice Ages, and finally the River Goyt carved out the valley as it exists today.

The river used to flow unimpeded through the valley to emerge at the northern end on its journey to Whaley Bridge and beyond as far as Stockport, where it joins with the River Tame to form the mighty Mersey. However, it was dammed in the first half of the 20th century to form the Fernilee and Errwood Reservoirs. The valley is bounded on the western side by a ridge from Shining Tor to Windgather Rocks, which forms the current county boundary between Cheshire and Derbyshire. On the eastern side is Combs Moss and Burbage Edge, overlooking Buxton a few miles to the south-east.

Fernilee Reservoir in the Goyt Valley

The upper stretches of moorland at the head of the valley are designated a Site of Special Scientific Interest, home to a wide range of native grasses and heathland plants like bilberry and crowberry, as well as upland birds including golden plover, red grouse, curlew and merlin. There are pockets of ancient oak, pine and birch woodland in the valley, as well as newer conifer forests, and grasslands around the reservoirs that are kept short by grazing sheep.

Ancient history

There is evidence for Neolithic farming in the Goyt Valley; the earliest inhabitants cleared the native woodland that once covered the landscape, and later the moors were burned and drained to provide rough pasture. The Romans were also active in the area, although the local belief that a Roman road, The Street, ran through the valley is disputed. However, the road that runs alongside the present-day Errwood Reservoir and up the western ridge to Pym Chair bears this name, suggesting a connection in local memory at least.

The River Goyt once formed the westernmost boundary of the Royal Forest of the Peak, 180 square miles of land that was forfeited to the Crown in 1155 to become a royal hunting preserve. This was not a forest in the modern sense of the word; some areas were certainly wooded, but it also included settlements, homesteads and cultivated land. It was governed outside English common law, with stern restrictions on game and hunting rights and severe penalties for poachers. The centre of administration and governance was Peak (or Peveril) Castle in Castleton in the Hope Valley, inhabited by the High Steward.

The origins of the river's name are unclear. Royal Forest records from 1285 list the watercourse as the River Gwid or Gwyth, likely from the Welsh 'gwyth' (channel or vein). The word 'goyt' seems to have Celtic or eve pre-Celtic origins, and 'goit' is an old Derbyshire dialect word for a stream or watercourse; it is possible that the two sources both contributed to form the name that is attached to the river today.

The valley once contained the hamlet of Goyt's Bridge, now lost beneath the waters of the Errwood Reservoir, but the village of Fernilee, on Long Hill at the northern end of the valley, escaped inundation, as did the tiny settlement of Taxal, north along the Goyt towards Whaley Bridge.

Industrial history

From the earliest times the valley has been used for agriculture, mainly sheep farming. At the height of the agricultural activity in the valley there were around 15 farms mainly engaged in sheep husbandry; the valley was the original home

Dale O'Goyt sheep on the moorland above the Goyt Valley

of the hardy Dale O'Goyt sheep, first referenced around 1770 and developed by local breeding into the Derbyshire Gritstone, one of the oldest native sheep breeds in Britain. The Gritstone is sturdy, resistant to disease and bred for the rugged High Peak countryside, and is now found across Derbyshire, Lancashire, Cheshire and Yorkshire, as well as in the mountains of Wales, Scotland and the Borders.

Coal mining took place on a small scale in the valley, particularly around Goyt's Moss and Derbyshire Bridge. Records of mining in the Goyt Valley date back to around 1600, but the quantity of coal in the valley was small enough and the terrain was difficult enough that the area never warranted significant commercial extraction. The coal mined in much of the valley was of sufficient quality for industrial use, but it was sulphurous and contained iron pyrite which made it smoky and smelly. It was therefore mostly unsuitable for domestic use with the exception of the House Coal Seam near Buxton, which had the extra advantage of easy transport into the town.

There was also a private domestic coal mine at Castedge on the grounds of Errwood Hall, recorded as early as 1811 and continuing (with a short hiatus during World War I) into the 1930s when much of the other mining activity in the area had ceased. Castedge Mine was a small operation employing only a handful of men, consisting largely of level tunnels (adits) and side galleries extending some 700 yards into the hillside, with a ventilation shaft near Shooters Clough. The tunnels were only 4 foot high, but a narrow gauge railway was laid to carry small wagons known as 'tubs'; these were pushed along the rails to transport coal to a covered loading area outside the mine, where it could be collected by local farmers or loaded onto a cart for delivery around the estate.

Goytsclough Quarry, near the re-sited packhorse bridge that once stood in the drowned hamlet of Goyt's Bridge, was first worked for gritstone in the 1670s by a local yeoman, Thomas Pickford, after his estates were confiscated by Cromwell for supporting the Cavaliers during the Civil War. There was once a huge water wheel here that was used to crush the stone before it was sent for use in road-mending and turnpike construction.

Pickford later began to transport flagstones to London, sending them south in packhorse trains. However, realising that it was uneconomic for the trains to return empty, around 1695 he started to offer a service transporting goods for third parties on the homeward journeys. Thus Pickford's removal and storage company was born, still very much in business and one of the UK's oldest companies.

Near Goytsclough Quarry are the remains of a paint factory. At the height of its activity in the later 19th century the factory employed over 20 people, bringing in barytes from Ladmanlow via the Cromford and High Peak Railway to be crushed and sold for use in making paint. The mill was powered by water from the stream in nearby Deep Clough.

There is also a history of gunpowder manufacture in the area, stemming back as far as the 16th century; this was used by the local mining and quarrying industries, but local legend has it that powder from the Goyt Valley was employed in the battle against the Spanish Armada in 1588. The Fernilee Gunpowder Mill, later the Chilworth Mill, was a major employer in the valley, powered by the River Goyt and boasting its own first aid team, fire fighters, a small-gauge tramway and even an orchestra.

Gunpowder manufacture was a risky business; the buildings had thick heavy walls but comparatively flimsy roofs to direct blasts upwards rather than outwards, and careful precautions were taken – for example, the workforce wore 'powder dresses', loose non-flammable clothing with bone buttons, and rubber footwear with copper nails to avoid the possibility of sparks from iron boot nails on cobbles.

Nevertheless there were frequent accidents at the Chilworth factory, and a number of fatalities. One of the worst occurred in August 1909, not long before the factory closed in 1921, when three men were killed in an explosion caused by a piece of grit or small metallic object that had found its way into the water-powered grinding mill. The site of the factory is now lost beneath the waters of Fernilee Reservoir.

Opposite top: The lost hamlet of Goyt's Bridge, now beneath Errwood Reservoir
Left: Shrine to the Blessed Virgin Mary, Goyt's Lane **Right:** Errwood Cottage, Goyt's Bridge

Transport links

Accessing the valley by road, the most popular route is along Goyt's Lane from Long Hill, the A5004 between Buxton and Whaley Bridge, which gives access to all the valley's car parks. Long Hill once formed part of the Buxton to Manchester turnpike, the earliest in Derbyshire, opening in 1725 and allowing easier travel north to Whaley Bridge and beyond. There was once an attractive white toll house in Fernilee, at the northern end of the valley; sadly this has not survived.

A second approach is from the A537 Buxton to Macclesfield road near the Cat and Fiddle, giving access only to the Derbyshire Bridge car park because of the one-way road following the river upstream from Errwood Reservoir. The A537 was once also a busy turnpike, opened in 1823 to replace the earlier route from Burbage on the outskirts of Buxton, descending to the head of Goyt's Moss and then climbing out again; this route was hilly and unsuitable for the increasing weight of traffic, so the A537 was created to replace it. A third road into the valley descends into the valley down the Embridge Causeway and The Street, giving access to The Street car park.

The narrow gritstone Derbyshire Bridge spans the River Goyt at the head of the valley, named for the fact that the Cheshire/Derbyshire boundary once followed the line of the river. This is no longer the case – since the 1920s the county line has followed the western ridge from Shining Tor to Windgather Rocks – but the name of the bridge has endured.

A little further down the valley, the old packhorse bridge used to be situated in the drowned hamlet of Goyt's Bridge, now lost beneath Errwood Reservoir to the north. When the valley was flooded the bridge was dismantled and reconstructed in its present position; these days it carries walkers, but originally it was used by packhorse trains carrying salt from Cheshire. The river crossing near the hamlet of Goyt's Bridge was known as Salters Ford, one of many such placenames that allow historians to map the ancient saltways across the high moorlands.

The Cromford and High Peak Railway was one of the earliest in the country, engineered by Josias Jessop and opened in 1831 to connect the Cromford Canal with the Peak Forest Canal at Whaley Bridge. The railway ran through the Goyt Valley, ascending the 1115-yard Bunsal Incline (now Goyt's Lane) where a stationary steam engine hauled wagons up and lowered them down. This section of the C&HPR closed in 1892, made obsolete by the opening of new lines between Hurdlow, Whaley Bridge and Buxton, and the rails were lifted shortly thereafter.

Derbyshire Bridge

The Grimshawes and Errwood Hall

One of the most beautiful and evocative features of the Goyt Valley is the ruined Errwood Hall, on the hillside above Errwood Reservoir. This beautiful Italianate mansion was built in 1845 by Samuel Grimshawe, a Manchester industrialist who lived in style and entertained on a grand scale. In 1835 the Grimshawe family bought most of the land in the upper Goyt Valley, including around 13 farms as well as cottages for labourers, villagers and farmhands; their coming was probably the most significant event in the valley in the 19th century, and they are still remembered fondly by the local people because of the prosperity and secure employment they brought with them.

Top: Errwood Hall, west front, c.1920s **Inset:** The King and Queen of Spain (seated) with Samuel Grimshaw's daugthers Mary and Genevieve in Biarritz

The hall itself was magnificently appointed and furnished, and the family hosted shooting parties on the moorlands as well as lavish social occasions and entertainments. They were very well connected, with friends among the English nobility as well as the Spanish royal family, alongside celebrities like Sir Charles Hallé, the founder of the Hallé Orchestra. Many of these would have visited Errwood to enjoy the Grimshawes' famed hospitality.

The family were no less generous to their servants and tenants; they employed a French chef, and the spreads laid on for the locals at Christmas were legendary. These were followed by carols, Spanish dancing (the butler, Mr Oyarzabal, was Spanish and a great local character), presents for the children and a hamper for each family.

The estate had its own coal mine at Castedge, and there was also a school for the estate children. This was set up by Dolores de Bergrin, a Spanish aristocrat who came to Errwood in 1883 after the death of Samuel Grimshawe to act as governess to the Grimshawe children and companion to Samuel's widow Jessie. She was greatly loved by the Grimshawe family and the estate workers; when she died in her mid-40s during a pilgrimage to Lourdes in 1889 a small Catholic shrine was built in her memory and dedicated to St Joseph. It still stands in the grounds of the hall, with fresh flowers left regularly on the altar.

Other retainers and members of the Grimshawe family were laid to rest in the family burial ground, on a hilltop above the hall. The family created an arboretum with the tree specimens brought home from their foreign travels, and the grounds were also adorned with 40,000 rhododendron and azalea bushes, which can still be seen around the ruins of the hall.

Sadly the Grimshawe family died out with Samuel's grandchildren, and the hall was compulsorily purchased and reduced to a ruin during the construction of Errwood Reservoir in the 1930s; it was above the waterline, but was destroyed along with farms and cottages to prevent pollution of the water. Nothing now remains except the foundations to floor level and a few sections of wall; these have been consolidated, forming a romantic and popular destination for walkers and visitors to the valley.

Errwood Reservoir

The Errwood and Fernilee Reservoirs

The twin reservoirs of Errwood and Fernilee lie in the northern end of the valley, constructed by the Stockport Corporation Water Undertaking to provide water for the town of Stockport and the surrounding area. Fernilee is the larger of the two, completed in 1938, with the upstream Errwood completed in 1968. Water for the reservoirs comes from a wide upland catchment area covering nearly 4,000 acres.

The construction of the reservoirs changed the face of the valley beyond measure, causing the destruction of 8 farms, 5 cottages, fields, the Chilworth Gunpowder Factory and the hamlets of Goyt's Bridge and Derbyshire Bridge. Many of the outlying buildings stood well above the proposed water line, but they were demolished as a precaution against pollution of the water supply; this was the fate of the stately Errwood Hall as well as a number of less grand dwellings.

Most of the farms in the upper valley were compulsorily purchased, with families relocating to new lives elsewhere; one farmer, Albert Warren of Fernilee Hall Farm, moved his entire operation to Warwickshire, including animals, implements, fixtures and fittings. The event, on 29 September 1932, was a community affair with the whole neighbourhood turning out to help load Mr Warren's horses, ducks, chickens, dogs and cattle onto a train at Whaley Bridge Station; it was even filmed by Pathé News.

A 'tin town' of temporary buildings was created near the village of Fernilee to house the reservoir construction workers. This would have been similar to the much larger settlement at Birchinlee, built during the construction of the Derwent and Howden dams in the Derwent Valley, with dormitories for single men and small huts for married men and families. These settlements were designed to be relatively self-contained; the larger ones offered shops, healthcare, schools, bathing facilities and a police presence. At the very least, though, the tin town at Fernilee would have had its own licensed premises, to keep the navvies out of the local drinking establishments and prevent problems with the residents.

Another piece of Goyt Valley history to be lost is the elegant suspension bridge that was constructed over the Fernilee Reservoir to maintain access across the valley on foot. This was insisted upon by the Grimshawe family as part of the compulsory purchase of their land, and it must have been an impressive sight. It was demolished in the 1960s when the construction of the Errwood dam provided alternative access and made it obsolete.

An experimental traffic scheme was introduced in the valley in the 1970s, closing roads and providing car parks and a mini-bus service to reduce tourist traffic at busy times. The legacy of this pioneering initiative can still be seen today, with plentiful car parking and parts of the valley kept traffic-free at peak visitor times.

The Goyt Valley today

On the bleak moorland road at the head of the valley, the Cat and Fiddle Inn is the second highest in England, 1,690 feet above sea level. The building is thought to have been erected by a Macclesfield banker and silk merchant, John Ryle, at the beginning of the 19th century. The origin of the inn's name is unclear – it is not thought to be related to the nursery rhyme 'Hey Diddle Diddle', but may derive from an early photograph of a cat and a violin given to the landlord by the Duke of Devonshire in the mid-19th century, from 'La Chatte Fidèle', a name given to a number of pubs in memory of faithful cats, or perhaps from 'Catherine la Fidèle' in memory of Catherine of Aragon, Henry VIII's first and longest-suffering wife. Whatever its provenance, the inn has long been a local landmark; at the time of writing this historic and unique site is home to Britain's highest whisky distillery.

There is a local legend that Pym Chair, a high point on the western ridge between Cats Tor and Windgather Rocks, was named for a highwayman who lay in wait there for travellers on the road below. Another story suggests that Pym was a Nonconformist preacher who addressed his flock at this isolated spot to avoid the authorities. However, the stories agree that there was once a chair-shaped rock here that may have been used by either the highwayman or

Windgather Rocks

the preacher. Sadly no trace of it remains today; it was apparently broken up and used for road-mending in the mid-19th century. The location still commands fine views, however, and the challenging climb out of the valley and up The Street to this point is popular among cyclists.

In fact there is a plethora of walking and cycling routes around the valley, taking in a variety of terrain from woodland and waterside paths to rugged moorland, with Windgather Rocks providing opportunities for climbers. The reservoirs are managed by United Utilities, offering sailing, walking and fishing; the Errwood Sailing Club was formed in 1968, shortly after the construction of the reservoir, and offers recreational sailing, racing, and training in sailing and powerboating at all levels.

One of the most significant modern land uses in the valley is the conifer forests planted by the Forestry Commission from the 1960s. The wider landscape around the valley is undergoing a ten-year conservation programme to restore nearly 2,500 acres of peatland; the programme involves farmers, landowners, local authorities and Natural England, and aims to conserve natural and archaeological features and habitats in a sustainable way.

Walk 3: Goyt's Lane - Burbage

Essential Information

Start: Goyt's Lane Car Park

Public Transport: None

Facilities: None

Car Park: Goyt's Lane, accessed from the A5004 Long Hill, between Buxton and Whaley Bridge. Also via minor roads through Kettleshulme, Rainow or Bollington.

Distance: 5 ½ miles

Path Description: Mostly footpaths and tracks over moorland and quiet lanes.

About the Walk

Our walk takes us from the reservoir close to the head of Bunsal Incline and within 100 yards of the site of its engine house. We explore the rugged moorland of the Goyt Valley and consider the changes to the landscape caused by heavy industry and the creation of the reservoirs in the valley.

Fernilee Reservoir opened in 1937 and Errwood Reservoir in 1967, both built by the Stockport and District Water Board. Both reservoirs covered areas of industry and residence, necessitating the diversion of roads and paths. It was once thought that a Roman road crossed the valley and ascended the bank on the western side of the valley via The Street; that theory is now disputed, but ancient salt roads and packhorse routes did pass this way. The packhorse bridge that once crossed Wildmoorstone Brook near the now submerged hamlet of Goyt's Bridge was relocated above the reservoir and will be passed on this walk.

Also visible across the valley are the remains of quarrying and the site of Goytsclough Mill, noted on the first edition OS 6" map of 1881 as a paint mill.

Overlooking Ladmanlow we see evidence of another local industry, namely coal mining; the hillside is pockmarked by shafts and the remains of such workings. The coal in this area sulphurous and unsuitable for domestic use, which meant that better transport links, initially via the Cromford and High Peak Railway, and access to more distant coalfields offering a higher quality product brought the closure of the local mines.

The section of the Cromford and High Peak Railway between Hurdlow and Whaley Bridge commenced operation on 6th July 1831. Built on similar principles to the canals it connected, the railway hugs the contours of the land and has gentle gradients except for the rope-worked incline planes, where stationary engines were employed to haul wagons up the gradients counterbalanced by those descending. The line between Ladmanlow and Whaley Bridge was abandoned on 27th June 1892 when all traffic was diverted via Buxton.

Goyt's Lane

Directions

1. Starting at the complex interface between many paths and the current Goyt's Lane, there is a free-standing gate *(see photo above)* and beyond it a public footpath fingerpost inscribed "Wildmoorstone Brook". Go through the pedestrian gate and follow the path as it descends steeply for just shy of a third of a mile.

2. At Wildmoorstone Brook, follow the fingerpost to Goytsclough Quarry by crossing the brook via a metal bridge and follow the well-made track along the left bank of the stream. The track rises as it follows Wildmoorstone Brook, but its way is blocked by a gate after around 250 yards. To the right of the track is a pedestrian gate, through which you should pass.

3. Continue along this straight section of track, via a further gate, for around 300 yards. Looking out over the water, it is now hard to imagine the valley as it once was. Goyt's Lane once meandered between the buildings of Goytsbridge Farm, crossing the valley floor via Goyt's Bridge with Goytshead Farm and Errwood Cottage both in close proximity. All were swept away with the creation of the reservoir.

4. Proceed along the track as it bends sharply to the left and begins to follow a wall line on your right.

5. As the track continues to the left to make its way uphill onto the moor, leave its hard surface and follow the wall line on your right, signposted to Goytsclough Quarry.

6. Descend to and cross the footbridge a short distance downhill from the track, maintaining the wall line on your right.

7. Around 150 yards from the footbridge the path crosses to the reservoir side of the wall. Follow the path for approximately

350 yards as it weaves along the hillside, keeping the wall within a few yards to touching distance on your left.

8. For the next half mile or so we cross land that is boggy even during dry spells. Cross the broken wall that makes its way to the valley floor below, and maintaining a distance of around 120 yards from a wall to your left, continue for 200 yards to a further broken wall.

9. Beyond the remains of the wall, which also descends to the valley floor, pick your way across the next third of a mile through heather moorland and brush, utilising the duck boards and board walks that have been placed to prevent further erosion of the land, as far as a fingerpost for Goytsclough Quarry and Derbyshire Bridge. The car parks on the opposite side of the valley now occupy the site of Goytsclough Quarry. The water running down the hillside into Goyt's Clough is a diversion of the stream running through Deep Clough that once powered the now demolished Goytsclough Mill (paint factory) on the opposite side of the road. The stone bridge you see to your right, in the valley bottom, is the former packhorse bridge from Goyt's Bridge that was moved to its current location when the valley was flooded.

10. Continue along the side of the valley for just shy of a third of a mile, signposted for Derbyshire Bridge, initially gaining a little height before descending into the valley beside a footbridge.

11. With the footbridge on your right, follow the path signposted for Berry Clough, ascending the hillside and keeping the stream on your right-hand side for around half a mile.

12. Follow the path as it crosses the stream and continues to ascend, leaving the water course to your left.

13. Take the left-hand of the two paths, signposted Burbage, as you maintain your course uphill for around 350 yards.

14. Immediately beyond the crest of the hill you descend to a wall, where a pedestrian gate has been provided for access to the field beyond. Cross the field to the right-hand edge of Burbage Edge Plantation, the lightly wooded area in front of you. The tranquillity of these open moors makes it difficult to envisage the huge amount of heavy industry that once took place here in order to exploit the natural resources beneath your feet.

15. Follow the edge of the wood round to your left, with views of Burbage, Harpur Hill and Buxton ahead. The embankment along the valley side to your right and below the busy Macclesfield Road once carried a spur of the Cromford and High Peak Railway to Goyt Colliery. Directly beneath the edge on which you stand is the route of the original turnpike to Macclesfield. Follow the path as it descends to the old turnpike, beside the bridge over the old railway formation.

16. Turn left onto the former turnpike and immediately cross the infilled bridge. The building on your left, beyond the bridge, is described as a Post Office Repeater Station. Continue down Macclesfield Old Road for 250 yards or so.

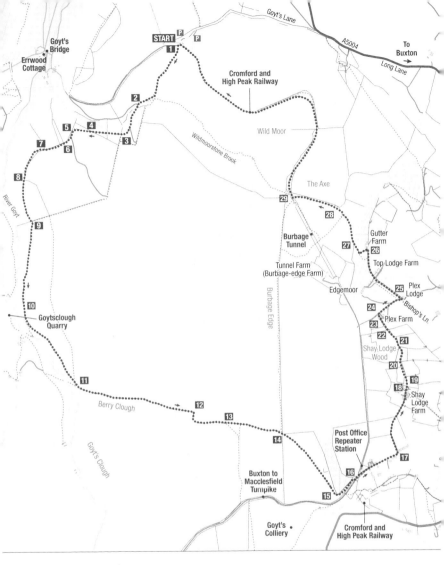

17. Opposite Level Lane and just prior to No. 140, turn left up a track to Shay Lodge Farm.

18. Keep straight ahead through the yard of Shay Lodge Farm, passing between the buildings and following the yellow painted arrows to a stile to fields, just beyond a small stone outbuilding.

19. Follow the path across three fields, crossing two more stiles before reaching the boundary of Shay Lodge Wood.

20. The wood is owned by Buxton Civic Association. Continue over the stile and into the wood, exiting via another stile into a field.

Plex Lodge

21. Keep the wall line to your right as you make your way towards Plex Farm.

22. With a paddock to your right, cross the stile ahead and continue through the field beyond.

23. At the gateway to the yard of The Barn at Plex Farm, cross the stile and continue ahead, passing the downhill side of the dwelling, along a metalled drive to a stile beyond.

24. After crossing the stile, turn immediately right to follow the lane down to Plex Lodge.

25. With Plex Lodge ahead, turn left up Bishop's Lane towards Edgemoor with its parkland, ponds and obelisk to admire. After passing the ponds, continue along the main drive for 250 yards, climbing the hill towards Gutter Farm and passing Top Lodge on your way.

26. Prior to Gutter Farm take the footpath on your left, which begins its ascent as a flight of steps. Beyond the steps the path zigzags up the hillside to a wall.

27. A pedestrian gate gives access to the moorland beyond. Beyond the gate the path continues to rise in the same general direction for around 200 yards, before beginning to descend and reaching a broken stone wall. This area of moorland bears the name "The Axe".

28. Follow the wall line down to the former trackbed of the Cromford and High Peak Railway.

29. On your left is Burbage Tunnel. At 580 yards this was the longest on the line between Whaley Bridge and Cromford. Turn right and follow the trackbed, which was abandoned in 1892, back to the car park just over a mile away.

Footpath along the former trackbed of the Cromford and High Peak Railway

Walk 4: Derbyshire Bridge, Cat and Fiddle and Goytsclough

Essential Information

Start: Derbyshire Bridge Car Park

Public Transport: The High Peak bus service 58 between Buxton and Macclesfield stops adjacent to the Cat and Fiddle.

Facilities: Toilets at Derbyshire Bridge. Distillery and café at the Cat and Fiddle. Peak View Tearooms at Stonway, a short distance from the route.

Car Park: Derbyshire Bridge, accessible via minor roads, off the A537 Buxton to Macclesfield road, between the Cat and Fiddle and Burbage.

Distance: 5 ½ miles

Path Description: Footpaths and lanes over moorland. Approximately a third of a mile on soft verges adjacent to the busy A537 (Cat and Fiddle road).

About the Walk

From the Derbyshire Bridge car park we traverse the old Buxton to Macclesfield turnpike to pass through the area once populated by the former community around Goyt Moss. Goyt Moss Farm was situated in the area of scrubland on the opposite side of the car park from the toilet block, a few yards towards Buxton. Moss Hall stood between the Derbyshire Bridge lane and the lane to Axe Edge, while Moss House was just upstream of the bridge carrying the Goyt under the old Macclesfield turnpike. Marchington Farm was a short distance further uphill, adjacent to the milestone, and would appear to have taken its name from the family of the same name who resided in Moss House at the time of the 1841 census.

We follow the former turnpike towards the Cat and Fiddle and the toll gate at Stonway, before heading in the direction of Shining Tor and Stake Side. The 1841 and 1851 censuses tell us that John Marsden Wain, of Taxal parish, was the landlord of the Cat and Fiddle in those years, running the inn alongside his wife Priscilla. In 1851 they were joined by a 16-year-old servant, Elizabeth Bottoms of Fernilee. Later the Wains moved a short distance down the old turnpike road to farm at Moss House until John's death in 1892, Priscilla having predeceased him by some 15 years.

Descending over the moorland, our path takes us past the site of Goytsclough Farm, mill and quarry. Goytsclough saw many tenants over the years with occupations such as agricultural labourer and gamekeeper. Thomas Braddock of Disley, born c.1839, lived there and was recorded as a gamekeeper in the 1891, 1901 and 1911 censuses, and his son James, born c.1890, lived next door at the same named address in 1911. James was also a gamekeeper and farmer. At the nearby cottages two generations of the Swindells family mined coal around the turn of the century.

We cross the Goyt via the resited packhorse bridge that once served those plying their trade on the ancient way between the salt-producing Cheshire Plain, Buxton and beyond; before the construction of the Errwood Reservoir the original location of the bridge was a mile downstream. We return to Derbyshire Bridge car park via Berry Clough and the former turnpike, where evidence of coal mining is writ large across the landscape. Let your eye follow the line of large depressions across the moors and you will notice the sites of two engine houses, both serving Thatch Marsh colliery.

The resited packhorse bridge

Left: Milestone on the old turnpike road **Right:** Far-reaching views towards Cheshire with Shutlingsloe on the horizon

Directions

1. From the entrance to Derbyshire Bridge car park, turn left along the former Buxton to Macclesfield turnpike and after around 300 yards pass the lane to Axe Edge on your left. Continue uphill towards the Cat and Fiddle for just over three quarters of a mile. Not far from the Axe Edge lane, just beyond the bridge under which the Goyt flows was Moss House, with a number of long-gone outbuildings beyond. Further along and less than 200 yards short of the junction with the A537, the turnpike once curved to the right to cross the moorland behind where the Cat and Fiddle now stands. Continue along the road to the junction.

2. At the busy A537, turn right towards the Cat and Fiddle, less than 250 yards away.

3. Continue along the A537 for a further 300 yards after the Cat and Fiddle to take the lane on your right, rejoining the former turnpike road.

4. After a short distance the tarmac gives way to a roughly cobbled surface. A further 100 yards along on your right is a milestone indicating 6 miles to Macclesfield and 164 to London. 80 yards further is the Peak and Northern Footpaths Society sign No. 429 and a track leading to Peak View Tearooms and the former Stonway quarry.

5. Bear right along the main path as it ascends the moors, coming to a gate after around 200 yards.

6. With the farm at Stake visible below and to your left, continue for a third of a mile to the end of the hard surfaced track.

7. Where a wall crosses the path, turn right and follow the wall on your left downhill for around a third of a mile, over the moor. At the tree line on your left, the wall follows the plantation boundary. Follow the path downhill at an increasing distance from the wall, as the vegetation begins to change in the more sheltered environment of Stake Clough, to reach a fingerpost indicating your way to Goytsclough Quarry.

8. Follow the direction of the sign for 300 yards or so, maintaining contact with a boundary fence and an increasingly dilapidated wall line.

9. Cross the stile and descend into the coniferous plantation and Deep Clough.

10. Cross the footbridge, noting the redundant water management features on your left, turning left immediately beyond the bridge.

11. Ascend the short rise, at the top of which you should take the left-hand fork in the path to follow the side of Deep Clough. However, before you do so, look to your right to see the remains of Goytsclough House.

12. Follow the path around the hillside to find some dressed stonework in the hillside, where you should cross the former mill lade via the plank footbridge and descend through the area once occupied by Goytsclough Mill, a paint works and the quarry floor beyond.

13. Cross the lane and descend the path opposite, which drops down to the River Goyt. Cross via the packhorse bridge, the original location of which was a mile downstream. Beyond the bridge turn left, ascending the hillside for 60 yards.

14. Turn right to follow the path for a quarter of a mile, up the valley towards Derbyshire Bridge.

15. Upon reaching a signpost pointing over a river footbridge to Stakeside, remain on the same side of the river and ascend Berry Clough for around half a mile.

16. Cross the stream, winding your way through the moorland landscape for 300 yards.

17. At the fork in the path, keep right signposted for Axe Edge. Follow this path without deviation for around a third of a mile until you reach a wide lane, beyond a number of coal pits.

18. Turn right to rejoin the former Buxton to Macclesfield turnpike and follow it back to Derbyshire Bridge, a distance of around three quarters of a mile.

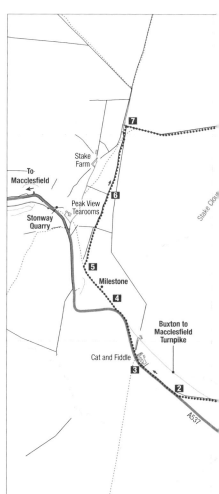

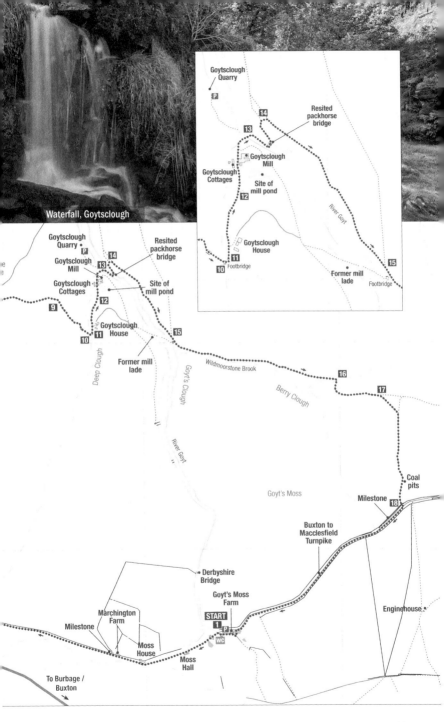

Waterfall, Goytsclough

Goytsclough Quarry

Resited packhorse bridge

14

13

Goytsclough Mill

Goytsclough Cottages

12

Site of mill pond

River Goyt

Goytsclough House

11

10 Footbridge

15

Former mill lade

Footbridge

Goytsclough Quarry

Resited packhorse bridge

14

13

Goytsclough Mill

Goytsclough Cottages

12

Site of mill pond

9

10 **11**

Goytsclough House

Deep Clough

Former mill lade

15

Goyt's Clough

Wildmoorstone Brook

16

17

Berry Clough

River Goyt

Goyt's Moss

Coal pits

Milestone

18

Buxton to Macclesfield Turnpike

Derbyshire Bridge

Goyt's Moss Farm

Enginehouse

START

1

P

WC

Milestone

Marchington Farm

Moss House

Moss Hall

To Burbage / Buxton

Walk 5: Errwood Hall

Essential Information

Start: Errwood Hall Car Park

Public Transport: None

Facilities: None

Car Park: Errwood Hall – please note, vehicular access to Errwood Hall car park is not permitted during summer Sundays and on bank holidays at specified times. See local notices for details. Walking to and from The Street car park along the reservoir road will add an additional mile to the overall distance.

Distance: 3 ½ miles (4 ½ miles from The Street car park)

Path Description: Well defined footpaths and tracks, a modest climb to St Joesph's Shrine.

About the Walk

This short walk takes you past the remains of Castedge Farm and the once grand Errwood Hall. We visit the Grimshawe family graves and venture out onto the open moors, passing the shrine of St Joseph and returning via Foxlow Edge, offering views down the Goyt Valley, Goyt's Moss and towards The Tors.

The ruins of Errwood Hall

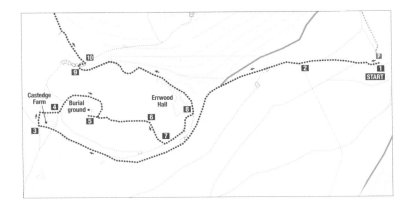

Directions

1. From the car park entrance, take the footpath almost opposite and ascend the hill, shortly passing an interpretation board. Follow the path to a wall 125 yards from the car park to a gap in the stone wall.

2. Continue up Shooters Clough, initially keeping the stream on your right. The distance from the wall line to the remains of Castedge Farm is around a third of a mile. After around 200 yards the old lane from Goyt's Bridge joins from the right. Around 125 yards further up the track the first of two tracks to Errwood Hall heads back up the hillside to your right. Shortly beyond, a lane once descended to your left, down the side of the clough to Castedge Mine which served the estate. The second track to Errwood Hall, shortly on your right, is graced by two substantial stone gate piers, while to your left, close to the valley bottom was the coal pit. Less than 200 yards along the track are the remains of Castedge Farm.

3. At Castedge Farm, turn right beyond the wall of the demolished building signposted for Foxlow Edge. Turn right again beyond the side wall of the farmhouse, rising behind the remains of the building for a few yards.

4. Turn left, following the path as it gently spirals up the hillside to the burial ground of the Grimshawes, their extended family, friends and servants. There was once a stone tomb at this hilltop site, noted on the OS maps as a vault. Following the abandonment of Errwood Hall the tomb became a magnet for treasure hunters and vandals alike, and as a result of their activities the tomb was sealed and the building was demolished.

5. After paying your respects, take the path ahead out of the fenced enclosure to descend towards Errwood Hall.

6. At a fork in the path, turn right, descending to a broader path that leads directly to the hall.

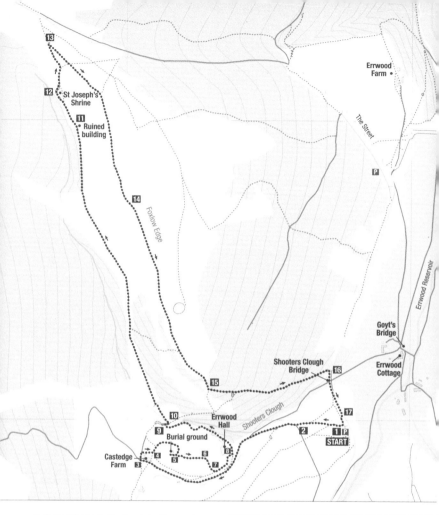

7. Turn left along the track to Errwood Hall, which is around 70 yards ahead. Errwood Hall was built under the supervision of Samuel Dominic Grimshawe around 1843; the 1851 census details Samuel, his wife Jessie, son Samuel, 8 servants and 1 visitor. The hall was demolished along with many of the estate farms in 1934, in order to protect the new reservoir from contamination.

Rhodedendrons near the hall

Estate workers posing beside the gates leadng to Errwood Hall, c.1880s

8. Turn left, passing close by the remains of the front door to Errwood Hall, and follow the track which becomes a path as you pass the ancillary buildings of the hall complex. The path follows a steep-sided clough, descending to a boardwalk.

9. A few yards beyond the boardwalk, turn right to ascend a short but steep flight of steps.

10. At the head of the steps, turn left, following the sign for Pym Chair, and continue for around half a mile.

11. Upon reaching the ruined stone walls of a structure (probably of agricultural origin), continue ahead and then take the left-hand path down to St Joseph's Shrine below.

12. Head up the steps beyond the shrine to rejoin the path you left in point 11, turning left and continuing for less than 200 yards to reach a fingerpost.

13. Follow the sign, doubling back on yourself, in the direction of Foxlow Edge. The path rises to follow the edge, coming to a crossing of a broken stone wall after around 650 yards.

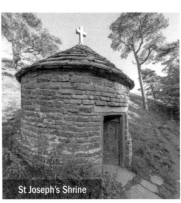
St Joseph's Shrine

14. Cross the wall line and continue along the path as it descends, keeping the stone wall on your right for 600 yards.

15. Cross the broken wall ahead, passing into the trees and following the path for a quarter of a mile down to the reservoir road.

16. Turn right, crossing Shooters Clough Bridge and following the road for 100 yards. (NB: If you parked at The Street car park, instead turn left here to walk back along the road to the start of your route.)

17. Turn right into Errwood Hall car park.

Walk 6: The Street – The Tors

Essential Information

Start: The Street Car Park

Public Transport: None

Facilities: None

Car Park: The Street, accessed from the A5004 Long Hill, between Buxton and Whaley Bridge. Also via minor roads through Kettleshulme, Rainow or Bollington.

Distance: 7 miles

Path Description: Well defined footpaths and tracks over moorland. There is a steady climb up Shooters Clough. Exposed path from Shining Tor to Pym Chair.

About the Walk

We begin this walk skirting the western bank of Errwood Reservoir. Climbing through woodland we pass the site of Errwood Hall and examine the remains of its two closest estate cottages, Castedge Farm and Shooters Clough Cottage, before continuing our ascent and passing evidence of the area's coal mining history. Out on the moors and tors the vistas open up, affording views across the Cheshire plain to the distant Welsh hills. The two miles along the exposed tors can be a little bracing, but the landscape more than makes up for any temporary discomfort. We return via an off-road path to one side of Embridge Causeway and The Street.

Directions

1. From The Street car park, head for its lower right-hand edge, walking in parallel with the lane to Derbyshire Bridge that skirts the western bank of Errwood Reservoir.

2. Take the grassy path for around 500 yards, in parallel to the lane towards Derbyshire Bridge.

3. Upon joining the lane, continue in the same general direction, shortly crossing Shooters Clough Bridge. 125 yards beyond the bridge on your right is Errwood Hall car park. To your left is the drowned settlement of Goyt's Bridge.

4. Turn right into the car park, taking the footpath almost opposite the vehicle entrance to ascend the hill, shortly passing an interpretation board. Continue up the path to a wall 125 yards from the car park.

5. Follow the path ahead up Shooters Clough, initially keeping the stream on your right. The distance from the wall line to the remains of Castedge Farm is around a third of a mile. After around 200 yards the old lane from Goyt's Bridge joins from the right. Around 125 yards further up the track the first of two tracks to Errwood Hall heads back up the hillside to your right. A little further on, a lane once descended to your left, running down the side of the clough to the Castedge coal mine. The second track to Errwood Hall, a little further along on your right, boasts two substantial stone gate piers. On your left and close to the valley bottom was the coal pit, and less than 200 yards further along the track are the remains of Castedge Farm.

6. At Castedge Farm, turn left and follow the path for around 350 yards as it continues up Shooters Clough. 150 yards beyond Castedge Farm and on your left lie the remains of Shooters Clough Cottage.

7. Upon reaching the ford, cross the stream and head back along the opposite bank of Shooters Clough for 175 yards, signposted Stakeside, where the track once more doubles back on itself to ascend the steep-sided clough.

Shining Tor

8. Follow the cobbled track along the wall line to your left, again heading away from Errwood Hall and signposted Stakeside, for just shy of 400 yards as far as the next hairpin. What looks like a dew pond around 20 yards from the hairpin bend in the track is in fact an old pit shaft.

9. Two marooned stone gateposts mark the entrance to the track as it switches back to continue its ascent, rising for 200 yards to a stone wall and the open moorland of Stake Side beyond.

10. After passing through the gap in the wall, fortified by a length of wooden fence and a gateway, turn right following the sign for the Cat and Fiddle for three quarters of a mile, as far as the point where the OS second edition 25" map describes two small buildings as a Shooting Box. Take advantage of the shelter afforded by the east face of a substantial wall on your right as you ascend Stake Side.

11. Turn right to follow a path that descends then snakes uphill as it ascends to Shining Tor.

12. At Shining Tor, with its triangulation point beyond the wall and bench carved with words of thanks to the park rangers who look after the area, turn right, following the fingerpost's direction to Pym Chair along a path made initially of stone slabs. 140 yards beyond is the Peak and Northern Footpath Society sign No. 200, which directs you towards Kettleshulme. Half a mile further on a path joins from Errwood Hall on the right.

13. Continue along the ridge-top causeway for 300 yards, to where a broken wall crosses the moor to your right.

14. Keep to the path which shadows the wall to your left for a further 500 yards, crossing another broken wall line. Around 250 yards along this section, look to your left and down into the valley floor to see the remains of Thorsbitch, a farm so isolated that little remains of the lane that must have been a lifeline to the residents. The farm is consistently documented in the census returns as Thors Batch or Thorsbatch, rather than the OS interpretation of Thorsbitch. In 1841 a 78-year-old farmer, Thomas Massey, his daughter Frances Cookson and his grandson John were tending the land. Mr Massey was still in charge of 40 acres a decade later, with his daughter, grandson and labourer Joseph Goddard all resident. By 1861 John Cookson was head of the household, looking after 75 acres with his two sisters and his 5-year-old nephew. Ten years later Mr Cookson had increased the size of his farm to 89 acres, living there with his sister Mary, nephew Edwin and farm labourer Peter Lomas. The farm was still in the same hands in 1881, now 75 acres, but by the 1891 census John Hibbert and his family had been installed. John's son James Hibbert was the sole resident ten years later in 1911. The valley carries Todd Brook which feeds Toddbrook reservoir, now famous for the partial collapse of the dam wall in August 2019.

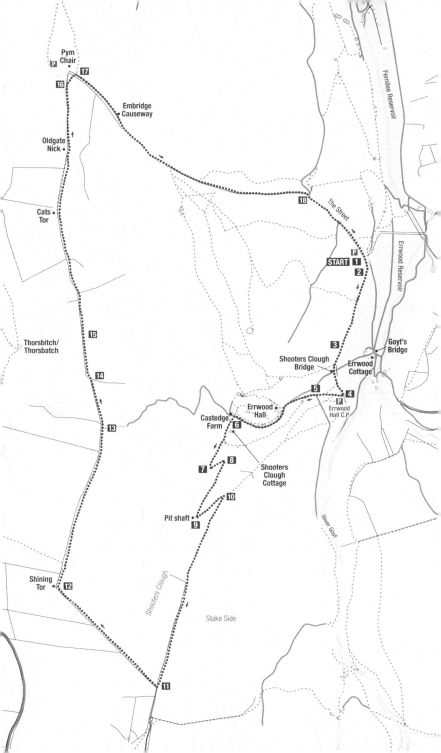

Looking towards Cats Tor from the moorland footpath

15. Maintain your way along this well-trodden path, reaching Cats Tor after 400 yards and Oldgate Nick a further 450 yards beyond. After surmounting the rise above Oldgate Nick you start the descent towards the lane known as Embridge Causeway.

16. 60 yards short of the lane, with Pym Chair car park in sight ahead, bear right at the fingerpost directing you to Windgather. Some legends have it that Pym was a highwayman who used this remote landmark to ambush travellers, while other tales suggest Pym was a Nonconformist preacher who used this open-air location to avoid the religious authorities. Perhaps they were one and the same.

17. Cross Embridge Causeway and the wall beyond. Immediately make a right turn to follow the path that runs in parallel with Embridge Causeway. Descend for a mile to the path's end, where a forestry track crosses to your left into the plantation of Hoo Moor.

18. Cross The Street, following the parallel path for 450 yards back to the car park where this walk started.

Walk 7: The Street – Taxal

Essential Information

Start: The Street Car Park

Public Transport: None

Facilities: None

Car Park: The Street, accessed from the A5004 Long Hill, between Buxton and Whaley Bridge. Also via minor roads through Kettleshulme, Rainow or Bollington.

Distance: 7 miles

Path: Undulating terrain over tracks, lanes and fields.

About the Walk

This walk begins by descending to the old lane to Fernilee alongside the reservoir of the same name. Continuing past Knipe, we drop to the valley floor and Hillbridge and Park Wood nature reserve.

Next we take a brief look at Taxal with its church of 12th century origin, before descending once again to the River Goyt and our turning point. Our return route follows the opposite bank of the Goyt from our outward journey. We pass a number of Water Board assets and walk along the former trackbed of the Cromford and High Peak Railway to the foot of Bunsal Incline, returning to The Street via the base of Errwood Dam.

Hillbridge and Park Wood

59

The River Goyt

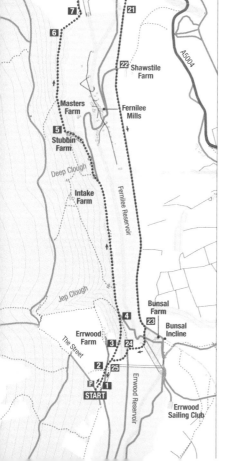

Directions

1. From the car park, cross The Street taking the footpath across the grassy bank between The Street and Goyt's Lane, to a pedestrian gate adjacent to the dam wall.

2. Once through the clappergate, take the right-hand path and after a few yards continue ahead for 100 yards to the tree line, rather than taking the right-hand path that descends steeply. 100 yards ahead and to your left once stood Errwood Farm, the residence of the Grimshawe family during the construction of Errwood Hall.

3. Pass through the clappergate and follow the path as it descends to the bank of Fernilee Reservoir.

4. Turn left and follow the broad path, formerly the lane from Derbyshire Bridge to Fernilee, for around three quarters of a mile, at which point the path rises steeply away from the reservoir. Around half a mile along the bank, Deep Clough descends the valley side. Not far above was the former site of Intake Farm. On your right the lane to Masters Farm and Fernilee Mills descended, and at the top of the path to the left of the junction with a track was the farmhouse and outbuildings of Stubbin Farm.

5. Turn right along the track for a quarter of a mile, signposted Fernilee.

6. Beyond a gate, turn right down the metalled lane for 150 yards to the dam wall.

7. Keep left to follow the metalled lane to Knipe Farm, just shy of half a mile away. The lane is gated with cattle grids, but pedestrian gates have been provided.

8. At Knipe Farm, turn back on yourself and walk along the drive in front of the house, continuing through the gate at the other side of the yard. Knipe Farm was the home of the Brocklehurst family, who were documented as living here in census returns from 1841 through to 1911.

9. Descend the hillside via a grass track, which becomes a holloway for a short distance.

10. Cross the stream via the footbridge beside a ford. After a few yards negotiate the stile, and then almost immediately turn left through the pedestrian gate into Hillbridge Wood nature reserve.

11. Continue along the path through the grassland into the woods, following the path as it rises for around 400 yards and crossing a stream as you go. The open

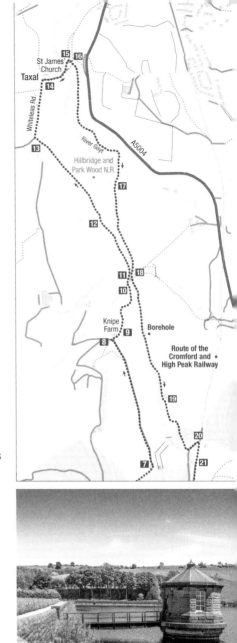

Fernilee Reservoir

A snowy view of the River Goyt at Hillbridge, c. 1920s

section of the nature reserve is carpeted with bluebells in spring.

12. Emerging into a large field, maintain contact with the right-hand boundary for around 120 yards, passing stone stoops and piles of stone on your right before the path veers left to cut across the field down to Whiteleas Road some 350 yards away.

13. At Whiteleas Road turn right, shortly crossing a stream beyond which the lane rises steeply before gently descending to Taxal church. The distance between the footpath joining Whiteleas Road and St James' Church is just under a quarter of a mile.

14. Prior to the church and graveyard, turn right down the steep gradient of the restricted byway to the River Goyt. Follow the path left immediately prior to the ford, and cross the footbridge a short distance beyond.

15. Once across the Goyt, turn right, and then after a few yards turn left and back

on yourself to rise steeply up a track for a few yards.

16. Turn right and back on yourself again at a crossing of tracks to follow a broad path, simply labelled "public footpath", for around half a mile through woodland. Part-way through the wood a fingerpost confirms the route with a sign to Fernilee.

17. Emerging from the wood beside the Goyt, continue along the path for less than 400 yards, passing through a number of fields and crossing a stream beyond which is a cast plate of the Stockport Corporation Water Works denoting the diameter of a pipe below. Follow the path a short distance further to the Peak and Northern Footpath Society signpost No. 237.

18. Continue ahead towards Fernilee, exiting the field via the pedestrian gate which leads to a track, the surface of which changes from hardcore to become a metalled lane. After around 250 yards you will reach the Goyt Valley Borehole electricity substation on your left, and then 170 yards further along on your right Borehole A. A further 200 yards along the lane brings you to a tarmacked yard adjacent to a Water Board building and tank.

19. From the yard, take the roadway uphill towards Fernilee Reservoir signposted as a public footpath, following it for less than 400 yards.

20. At the barrier and junction with a lane, turn right to follow the lane 100 yards to the dam wall. On your immediate left is the route once followed by the Cromford and High Peak Railway.

21. Continue along the side of Fernilee Reservoir for around 350 yards. The grass track to the left of the metalled lane is on the former trackbed of the C&HPR.

22. At the end of the metalled lane, continue through the gate along the former railway formation for just under a mile to reach the foot of Bunsal Incline. Where you leave the metalled lane near Fernilee dam wall, a grass track meanders up the hillside to your left and the remains of Shawstile Farm can still be seen. Between 1841 and 1881 Shawstile/style was home to the Lomas family, who farmed between 140 and 170 acres. However, the fortunes of the farm appear to have taken a turn for the worse, since subsequent tenants/owners were labourers until the turn of the century. What cannot be seen, however, is the lane's old route to your right, down into the valley bottom to Fernilee Mills, once a hive of industrial activity with complex

St James' Church, Taxal

tram and water management systems for the production of gunpowder. The lane wound its way up the opposite bank, passing Masters Farm, once home to George Wilson and his extended family, to become the path we walked along at the beginning of our journey.

23. When you reach the bottom of the incline, go through the clappergate on your right and follow the path towards the dam wall, crossing the overflow on your way. Continue beneath the dam wall and up the steep path on the opposite side of the valley. To the left of the dam wall and close to the railway incline was Bunsal Farm.

24. Join a wide, well-surfaced path and turn left to continue uphill towards the top of the dam wall, keeping left as the path you followed earlier joins from the right.

25. Once through the clappergate, return to The Street ahead.

Bibliography

A History of the Peak District Moors by David Hey (Pen & Sword, 2014)

Bates's Baby: The Story of Buxton's Pavilion Gardens by Sheila Barker (published by the author, 2014)

Buxton: A Selection of 8 Walks by Louise Maskill and Mark Titterton (Bradwell Books, 2017)

Cotton Mills and Printworks on the River Goyt and its Tributaries by Stephen Lewis (Florence Publishing, 2014)

Derbyshire Black Marble by J.M. Tomlinson (PDMHS, 1996)

Derbyshire Watermills – Corn Mills by Alan Gifford (Midland Mills Group, 1999)

Fernilee Powder Mills by Joyce Winfield (published by the author, 1996)

Goyt Valley by Roland Smith (Peak National Park, n.d.)

Goyt Valley and its People by Gerald Hancock (published by the author, 1996)

Goyt Valley Miner: Errwood Hall and Castedge Pit by Kevin Dranfield (published by the author, 2008)

Goyt Valley Romance: Errwood Hall and the Grimshawes by Gerald Hancock (published by the author, 2001)

Peak Place-Names by Louis McMeeken (Halsgrove, 2003)

Peakland Roads and Trackways by Arthur E. Dodd and Evelyn M. Dodd (Landmark, n.d.)

Reading the Peak District Landscape by J. Barnatt (Historic England, 2019)

Some Aspects of the Glacial and Post-Glacial History of the Lower Goyt Valley, Cheshire by R. J. Rice (*Proc. Geologists Association*, 68(3), 1957)

The Goyt (The Forgotten Valley) and Errwood Hall by Gerald Hancock (published by the author, 2016)

The Buildings of England: Derbyshire by Nikolaus Pevsner (Penguin, 1953)

The Cromford and High Peak Railway by A. Rimmer (Oakwood Press, 1995)

The Cromford and High Peak Railway, revised edition featuring Wirksworth and Steeple Grange by John Marshall (Martin Bairstow, 2011)

The Goyt Valley (www.goyt-valley.org.uk/), a wonderfully informative and useful website maintained by David Stirling

The Industrial Archaeology of the Peak District by Helen Harris (Ashbourne Editions, 1971)

The Peak of Derbyshire: Its Scenery and Antiquities by John Leyland (Seeley & Co., 1891)

Turnpike Roads Around Buxton by A.F. Roberts (published by the author, 1992)